# Non Piangere Furbino!

# Don't Cry, Sly!

retold by

Henriette Barkow

illustrated by

Richard Johnson

Italian translation
by Paola Antonioni

La mamma di Furbino
gridava sempre:
"Metti in ordine la tua
stanza! Lava i piatti!"

Sly's mum was always shouting:
"Tidy your room! Do the dishes!"

"Spazzolati i denti! Spazzolati i
capelli!"
E per quanto Furbino facesse, per
la sua mamma non bastava mai.

"Brush your teeth! Comb your hair!"
And however much Sly did, it was never
enough for his mum.

Nella casa vicina, Piccola Rossa sentiva tutto. Odiava il modo
in cui la mamma di Furbino gridava e strillava sempre.

Next door Little Red could hear everything. She hated the way Sly's mum
always screamed and shouted.

Un giorno sentì un grido:
"Ho voglia di pollo arrosto!"
Piccola Rossa ebbe tanta,
tanta paura.

One day she heard a scream:
"I want roast chicken!"
And Little Red became very
very scared.

Anche Furbino si spaventò, non aveva mai preso una gallina;
ma essendo una volpe scaltra preparò un piano.

Sly was scared too, he'd never caught a hen before,
but being a smart fox he had a plan.

Quando Piccola Rossa uscì, Furbino entrò di nascosto in casa sua e aspettò il suo ritorno.

When Little Red went out Sly sneaked into her house and waited and waited, until she returned.

"Aiuto! Aiuto!" gridò Piccola Rossa quando vide Furbino, e saltò sopra la libreria.
Ma questo non era un problema per Furbino, dopotutto era una volpe con un piano.

"Help! Help!" Little Red cried when she saw Sly and jumped up onto the top of the bookcase.
But that was no problem for Sly, after all, he was a fox with a plan.

Furbino cominciò a girarsi e rigirarsi,
inseguendosi la coda. Andò sempre
più veloce finché…

Sly started spinning round and round, chasing his tail.
Faster and faster he went until…

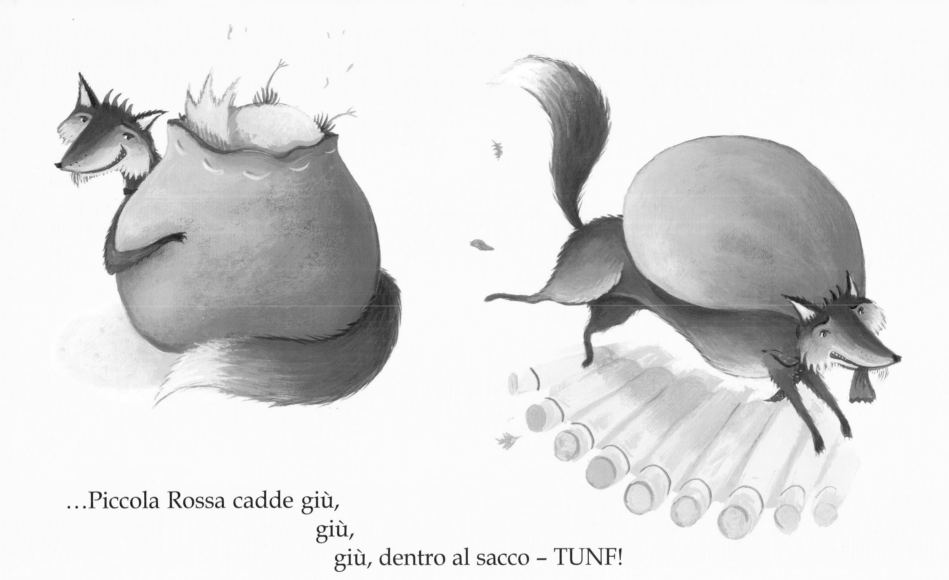

…Piccola Rossa cadde giù,
                giù,
                        giù, dentro al sacco – TUNF!

Furbino trascinò il sacco giù per la scala – TUNF, TUNF, BAM!

…Little Red fell down,
                down,
                        down into the sack - THUMP!

Sly dragged the sack down the stairs - THUMPADY, THUMPADY, BUMP!

Quando arrivò per terra era così stanco e
frastornato che si addormentò in fondo alla scala.

By the time he reached the ground he was so tired and
dizzy that he fell asleep at the bottom of the stairs.

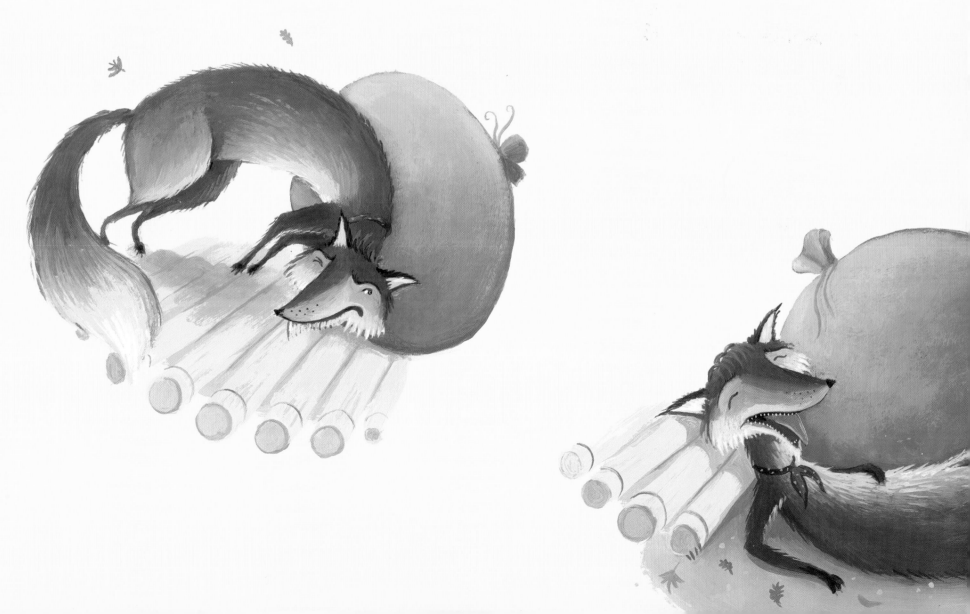

Now was Little Red's chance.

Ecco l'occasione che Piccola Rossa aspettava.

Si liberò dal sacco e corse velocemente su, su per la scala.

She squeezed herself out of the sack and ran as fast as she could, up, up, up the stairs.

Quando Piccola Rossa si fu ripresa cominciò a pensare al povero Furbino
che si sarebbe trovato nei guai. Cosa poteva fare per aiutarlo?

When Little Red had recovered she thought about poor Sly and all the trouble
he would be in. What could she do to help?

Si guardò attorno in cucina e poi ebbe un'idea.

She looked around her kitchen and then she had an idea.

Quando ebbe finito, svegliò Furbino e gli spiegò il suo piano.

When she had finished she woke Sly and told him of her plan.

Furbino tornò a casa con il suo sacco pesante.
Preparò la cena, apparecchiò il tavolo e poi chiamò la sua mamma. "Vieni a mangiare, il pollo arrosto è pronto!"

Sly went home with his heavy sack. He made the dinner and set the table, and then he called his mum. "Roast chicken is ready, come and get it!"

E come gridò e strillò la mamma di Furbino!
Grida di piacere e di gioia: "Questa è la
cena più buona che io abbia mai mangiato!"

And did Sly's mum scream and shout?
She screamed with delight.
She shouted with joy: "That's the best
dinner I've ever had!"

Da quel giorno in avanti Furbino preparò tutti i pasti con l'aiuto
della sua nuova amica.
E la mamma di Furbino? Beh, lo stuzzicò solo di tanto in tanto.

From that day forth Sly did all the cooking with the help of his new friend.
And Sly's mum, well she only nagged him now and then.

To the children of Mrs Michelsen's Class of 02
at Moss Hall Junior School
H.B.

For my friends, Rebecca Edwards
and Richard Holland
R.J.

Mantra
5 Alexandra Grove, London N12 8NU
www.mantralingua.com